ABOUT this book

Have you ever wondered where shells come from? On every page, find out the answers to questions like this and other fascinating facts about the seashore. Words in **bold** are explained in the glossary on page 31.

Look and find

★ ★

limpet

All through the book, you will see the **Look and find** symbol. This has the name and picture of a small object that is hidden somewhere on the page. Look carefully to see if you can find it.

Now I know...

★ This box contains quick answers to all of the questions.

★ They will help you remember all about the amazing world of the seashore.

WHAT is a seashore?

All the land on Earth – every island and continent – has sea all around it. Where the land meets the sea, there is a seashore. And a seashore is not like other places because parts of it are underwater for some of the day, and uncovered at other times. Seashores provide a home for all kinds of interesting plants and animals.

Red-tailed tropic bird flying out to sea to fish

Green turtles come ashore to lay their eggs in the sand every two to four years.

That's Amazing!

Sea covers two-thirds of Earth's surface!

Around the Arctic and Antarctica the seashores are covered in snow and ice!

HOW are seashores different around the world?

Seashores are different depending on whether they are in a warm or cold place, how windy it is and what type of rocks form the land. Some seashores are just rocky ledges or tall cliffs. Some are tropical **mangrove swamps**. Others have beaches fringed with **coral reefs**. Beaches can also be sandy or covered in pebbles. Icy seashores are home to only a few animals such as penguins, but many different animals can live on warmer shores.

Rock pools are found on rocky shores. They are home to many different animals such as crabs.

WHERE can you find animals on the seashore?

Most seashore animals hide away in sheltered places. **Molluscs** and worms live on rocks or under the sand. Fish swim in the sea. Birds search for food along the shore and build their nests on cliffs. Sand dunes make a dry home for reptiles and insects.

Now I know...

★ A seashore is where the land meets the sea.
★ There are many different kinds of seashore around the world.
★ Animals on the seashore shelter in places where they can hide.

HOW are rocky and sandy shores made?

Nothing on the seashore is ever still. Waves break, the wind blows, and the tides go in and out. The wind and sea make the shape of the coastline. Waves pound against the cliffs and wear them away. Pieces of rock break off. They roll around in the sea and break up into pebbles. Then, pebbles slowly break down into smaller pieces called **shingle**. In time, shingle wears down into fine grains of sand.

WHAT makes pebbles different colours?

The pebbles on a beach come from many different kinds of rock. Their varied colours show what kind of rock. Some pebbles come from other parts of the coast and have been washed ashore by the sea.

Dunlin

WHY is the sea salty?

Seawater is salty because it has lots of different **minerals** mixed up in it. Some minerals are washed into the sea from rocks and soil. Others come from the remains of plants and animals that once lived in the sea.

That's Amazing!

In some places, the sand is black because it is made of lava from volcanoes!

On some seashores you can find fossils – the remains of animals that turned to stone millions of years ago!

A lighthouse is a tower with a bright light on top. The light warns ships away from rocky seashores.

Now I know...

★ The wind and sea wear away the coast to form rocks and sand.
★ Pebbles come from different kinds and colours of rock.
★ The mixture of minerals in seawater makes it salty.

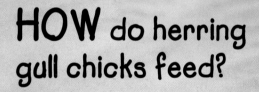
WHY do kittiwakes nest on cliffs?

Tall cliffs and rocky islands make safe nesting places for kittiwakes and other seabirds. Here, they are close to the sea and the fish they eat. But they are safely out of the reach of enemies, such as rats and foxes. Kittiwakes crowd onto rocky ledges to build their nests of seaweed and mud. Other birds build nests with sticks, or lay their eggs straight onto the rocks.

That's Amazing!

Guillemots lay eggs on cliff ledges only a few centimetres wide!

American bald eagles build the biggest bird nests!

HOW do herring gull chicks feed?

Herring gulls catch fish, molluscs and crabs to eat. When a parent gull returns to the nest, the chick taps the red spot on its parent's beak. This makes the parent cough up the mushy food it has just eaten to feed the chick.

Herring gull feeding chick

8

WHERE do puffins lay their eggs?

Puffins nest on cliff tops in spring and summer. They dig holes in the soft **turf** with their large, stripy beaks. Or they lay their eggs in old rabbit **burrows**, where they will be safely tucked away. Puffins often stand guard near their burrows. When their eggs have hatched and the chicks have grown, the puffins fly out to sea for the winter.

Herring gull

Puffin

Gannets

Kittiwakes

Now I know...

★ Seabirds nest on cliffs where they are safe from enemies.
★ Herring gulls cough up food for their chicks to eat.
★ Puffins lay their eggs in burrows on the cliff tops.

Look and find ★ ★ sea pea

WHAT are sand dunes?

On wide, sandy beaches, strong winds often blow dry sand about. Sometimes the sand is blown towards tough grasses at the back of the beach. Then it can build up into hills called dunes. The grasses that grow on the dunes hold the sand in place with their spreading roots. As more sand piles up, the dunes grow bigger. A thin layer of soil builds up, so more plants grow. These attract many kinds of special animals.

Clouded yellow butterfly

Yellow horned-poppy

Grasshopper

HOW do plants survive on sand dunes?

Plants on sand dunes have to be tough, because the salt breezes and sun can be strong, and there is very little water. Most plants grow close to the ground and have long, spreading roots that hold them firmly in place. Many plants have fat, waxy leaves that will not dry out, or hairy leaves that trap tiny drops of water.

Greater bird's-foot trefoil

10

WHICH animals live there?

The grasses and flowers on dunes attract insects such as grasshoppers and butterflies. Lizards scuttle across the warm sand. Birds feed on insects in the daytime. Rabbits, toads, snails and mice come out to feed at night. Foxes begin hunting for **prey** in the evening when it is cooler. The tracks and trails of many animals can be seen across the dunes in the early morning.

Foxes and their cubs visit sand dunes in the evening to hunt for prey such as rabbits, insects and mice.

That's Amazing!

Marram grass grows faster if it is covered by sand!

If there were no plants to hold the sand in place, dunes would constantly move and change shape!

Butterflies are attracted to the sand dunes by the colourful flowers on which they feed.

Dark green fritillary butterfly

Marram grass

Sea milkweed

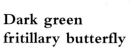

Silverweed

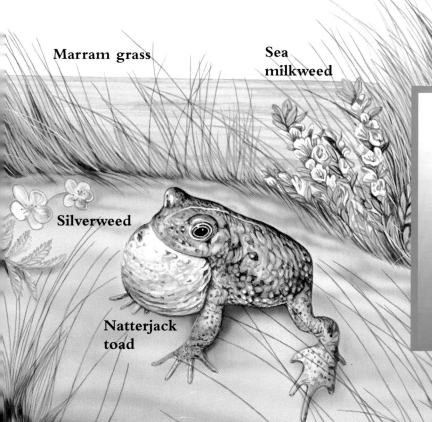

Natterjack toad

Now I know...

★ Dunes are hills of sand that form at the back of some beaches.

★ Dune plants have long roots and leaves that do not dry out.

★ Insects, lizards, toads, rabbits and foxes live on sand dunes.

HOW do jellyfish get stranded?

Look and find ★ ★ **cockle shell**

Along the seashore the **tide** comes in twice a day, then goes out again. At every high tide, seaweed and other objects are washed up onto the shore, then left behind as the sea goes out at low tide. A long wiggly line of seaweed and debris across a beach shows where the high tide line is. During storms, when the sea is rough, jellyfish are sometimes thrown ashore at high tide and left **stranded**.

That's Amazing!

Huge seeds of the coco-de-mer palm drift for thousands of kilometres!

The highest tides are at the Bay of Fundy in Canada. They can rise over 14 m (the height of a five-storey building)!

Herring gulls

Bladder wrack

12

WHERE do shells come from?

Shells once had small animals called molluscs living inside them. The hard shells protected their soft bodies. Some shells, such as whelks, are in one piece and some have coils. Others, such as mussels, have two halves joined together by a tiny hinge.

WHAT can you find on the high tide line?

On the beach there will be seaweeds, seashells, interesting bits of **driftwood**, sandhoppers, dead crabs and starfish. You may also find mermaid's purses (the egg cases of sharks and rays), and the skeletons of fish and birds. Be careful not to touch any stranded jellyfish, as they can sting you.

Common starfish

Stranded jellyfish

Mermaid's purse

Whelks

Sandhopper

Now I know...

★ Sea creatures are sometimes stranded on the seashore at high tide.

★ Shells once had molluscs living inside them.

★ You can find many different things along the high tide line.

WHY do lugworms live under the sand?

It is always cool and wet under the sand, so it makes a good hiding-place for animals that dig burrows. Molluscs, lugworms and many other creatures live in burrows under the sand. There, they are hidden from **predators** such as birds and crabs. The wet sand also keeps them from drying out in the wind and sun.

HOW do burrowers feed?

Molluscs come up to feed when the tide is in. They stick tiny feeding tubes out of their shells and suck up seawater. They **filter** out bits of food then pump out the water. Lugworms swallow sand as they burrow, eating any food they find. They squirt out the waste sand behind them, forming worm casts.

Worm cast

Sand dollar

Cockle

Pen shell

Lugworm

14

WHERE do purple sea urchins dig their burrows?

Purple sea urchins dig their burrows in solid rock. They gnaw at the rock with their

mouths and wiggle their tough spines around to scrape out a channel. They often get stuck in their burrows as they grow larger.

That's Amazing!

Razor shells can dig half of their shell into the sand in just one second!

A Californian sea urchin took 20 years to drill into a solid steel girder!

Piddock

Tellin

Razor shell

Now I know...

★ Lugworms and molluscs burrow under the sand to hide.

★ Burrowers have feeding tubes that filter food from seawater.

★ Purple sea urchins dig into rocks with their mouths and spines.

Look and find
anemone

HOW do oystercatchers catch their food?

As the tide goes out, wading birds move along the shore looking for food. Oystercatchers like to eat worms, and molluscs such as mussels. They use their sharp orange beaks to lever the molluscs off the rocks, and some hammer the shells with their beaks until the shells smash. Others use their beaks to pull the shells apart and reach the juicy flesh inside.

Turnstones flick pebbles over, looking for the shrimps and molluscs hiding underneath.

Oystercatcher

That's Amazing!

Godwits have super-sensitive beaks that can feel creepy crawlies moving in the sand or mud below them!

Plovers pretend to be hurt if their eggs or chicks are in danger, to lure enemies away from their nest!

WHY do curlews have such long beaks?

Wading birds have beaks that are just the right shape for poking into soft sand or mud to look for food. A curlew has a specially long beak to probe deep down into the sand to feel for worms and molluscs. Plovers and other birds with short beaks look for food near the surface of the sand or in the water. This means different birds can feed together, but do not compete for the same food.

WHERE do plovers lay their eggs?

Plovers live on pebbly beaches and lay their eggs in shallow hollows on the ground. Their eggs are pale and speckled like the stones around them, so they are well **camouflaged**. The mother bird's feathers also match her surroundings, so that enemies do not spot her as she sits on her eggs.

Curlew

Black-headed gull

Now I know...

★ An oystercatcher can open shells with its sharp beak.

★ A curlew's long beak helps it search for food in the sand.

★ A plover lays its camouflaged eggs in shallow hollows on pebbly beaches.

WHAT lives in a rock pool?

Look and find ★ ★ sea slug

Beneath the calm surface of a rock pool there is a busy underwater world. Seaweeds grow there, and all kinds of animals can hide and feed safely underwater when the tide is out. Molluscs and anemones cling to the rocks, crabs scuttle across the sand, and small fish swim to and fro.

A starfish wraps its arms around a shell and pulls it open so it can eat the animal inside.

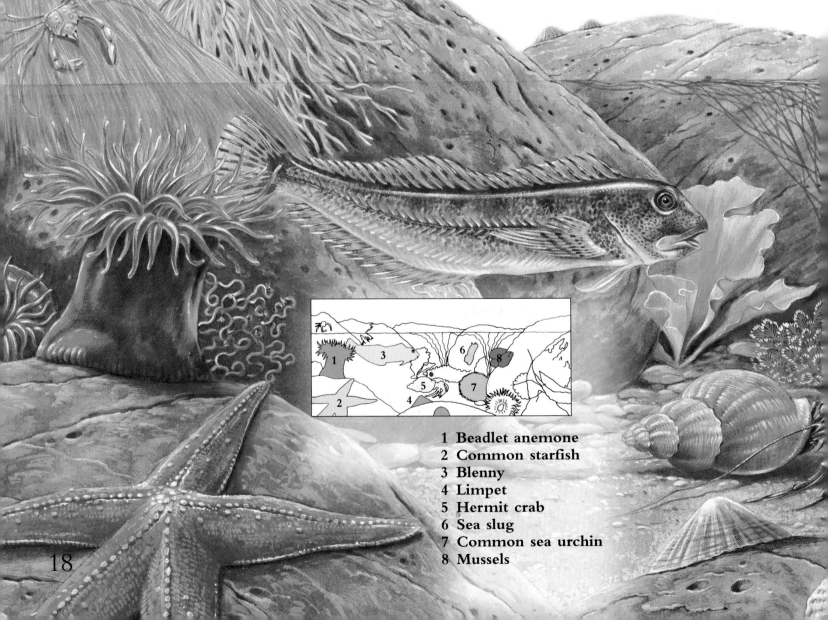

1 Beadlet anemone
2 Common starfish
3 Blenny
4 Limpet
5 Hermit crab
6 Sea slug
7 Common sea urchin
8 Mussels

18

WHY do limpets cling to rocks?

Molluscs have to be able to hold tightly onto rocks or they would be smashed by strong waves. A limpet seals itself onto rocks with a strong muscular foot, but can still move around. Mussels are attached to rocks by **byssus threads**. A barnacle cements itself to a rock and stays there all its life.

HOW do sea urchins eat?

Spiny sea urchins move across rocks by gripping on with thin tube feet that are like suckers. Their mouths are right underneath their bodies. Sea urchins graze on seaweeds and tiny plants. They eat by scraping plants off the rocks with their five powerful teeth.

That's Amazing!

Barnacles attract food by waving their feathery legs about!

Some sea urchins use pebbles, shells and seaweeds to disguise themselves!

Now I know...

★ A rock pool is a hiding place for many different sea animals.
★ Limpets cling onto rocks for safety.
★ Sea urchins eat using their powerful hidden teeth.

19

Look and find ★ fiddler crab ★

WHY do trees grow on stilts?

Seashores and **estuaries** in hot countries are often swampy and fringed with mangrove trees. These strange trees can grow in salty water. They have long roots like stilts that prop the trees above the mud and hold them in place. Mangrove roots stop the mud in which they grow from being washed away.

HOW does the archerfish catch its prey?

The archerfish can shoot down prey that is out of the water. It swims up below a leaf with an insect on it and squirts water at it. Taken by surprise, the insect falls into the water and the archerfish snaps it up.

Brown pelican

That's Amazing!

Mudskippers can stand on their tails and jump forward a metre at a time!

Some mangrove trees have leaves that sweat salt if they grow in very salty water!

American crocodile

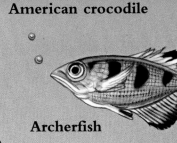

Archerfish

20

WHICH fish can climb and skip?

Mudskippers are small fish that can survive out of water for a long time. They have strong, stumpy front fins. They use them like legs to pull themselves across wet mud and to clamber up tree roots. Mudskippers can move quite fast. They skip over mud to catch their prey, and hop back quickly into the water if an enemy appears.

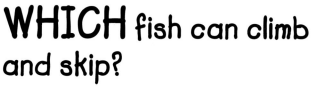

Mudskippers climb onto land to find prey such as insects, shrimps and worms.

Roseate spoonbill

Now I know...

★ Mangrove trees have roots like stilts that hold them in place.

★ Archerfish squirt water at insects to knock them down.

★ Mudskippers use their front fins like legs to climb and skip.

Look and find ★
★ whelk

WHY do crabs have claws?

Crabs use their claws to pick up food and tear it apart. They also use them as weapons to fight off attackers. Male crabs have larger claws than female crabs. Most crabs have tough shells like armour, to protect them from enemies. Even so, they are often eaten by shore birds, octopuses, and mammals such as seals and otters.

This crab has its claws up, ready to defend itself from attackers.

HOW do shrimps and prawns swim?

Shrimps and prawns swim over the seabed using the feathery legs on the back halves of their bodies like paddles. They can swim backwards by flicking their fan-shaped tails beneath them. As they swim, they pick up any bits of food they find using the claws on their two front legs.

Common prawns

22

WHERE do lobsters find their food?

Lobsters find their food in shallow water near the seashore. They usually hide during the day and come out to feed at night. They are **scavengers**, eating dead or dying fish and animals. Most lobsters live near one seashore all their lives. But some lobsters **migrate** to other seashores, probably to find a new place to feed.

Norway lobster

That's Amazing!

Each year, thousands of spiny lobsters migrate over 100 km in single file along the seabed near the coast of Florida, USA!

Hermit crabs do not have shells of their own, but move into empty seashells!

HOME SWEET HOME

Now I know...

★ Crabs use their claws to eat and to fight off attackers.
★ Shrimps and prawns swim using their back legs and tail.
★ Lobsters are scavengers that find food in shallow water.

Common shrimp

Look and find
★ sea snail ★

WHY are seaweeds slimy?

Seaweeds can be brown, green or red. Some are flat and thin, and others look like ferns or bootlaces. Seaweeds do not have leaves or flowers. Instead they have tough, leathery fronds. Many of them are naturally slimy, so they do not dry out in the sun when the tide goes out. Being slippery also stops them from breaking in rough seas.

WHERE does sea lettuce grow?

Bright green seaweeds, such as sea lettuce, grow high up on the shore. Red and brown seaweeds grow further down, near the low tide mark. Seaweeds also grow on rocks along the seashore and in rock pools. They cling to the rocks with root-like grippers called **holdfasts**.

That's Amazing!

Seaweed is used to thicken ice cream and even to make explosives!

Giant Californian kelp can grow 60 cm in a day and can be as long as 60 m!

1	Sea lettuce	7	Sugar kelp
2	Furbelows	8	Thongweed
3	Bladder wrack	9	Shore crab
4	Serrated wrack	10	Carragheen
5	Sea snail	11	Shrimp
6	Oarweed	12	Dulse

WHICH seaweeds can you eat?

Some seaweeds are chopped and cooked like a vegetable, or grated and eaten raw. A red seaweed called carragheen is used to make gel for jellies. Dulse is another red seaweed that is eaten as a vegetable. Some people also like to eat crinkly brown sugar kelp and a seaweed called laver.

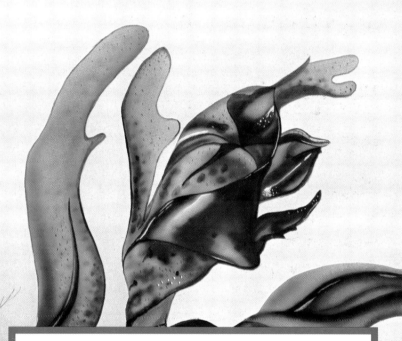

Now I know...

★ Seaweed is slimy, so it does not dry out and is not torn by waves.
★ Green seaweeds grow on rocks high on the seashore.
★ Some seaweeds are cooked and eaten like a vegetable.

WHICH fish live in the shallows?

Many different kinds of fish swim in the shallow water near the shore. Silvery sand eels, and fish such as blennies and gobies, swim just below the low tide mark. Scallops pump their way through the water. Jellyfish float about just under the waves, pipefish hide in eel grass, and sea urchins and starfish creep along the seabed looking for food.

That's Amazing!

Some flatfish can change colour to match the seabed!

Stonefish look like harmless pieces of coral, but their hidden spines are poisonous!

WHY do plaice disguise themselves?

The plaice is a flatfish. It lives on the seabed and keeps very still. To protect itself from enemies, it is the same colour as the ground on which it lies. It flips sand over itself with its fins to complete its camouflage, so it is very hard to spot.

HOW does a jellyfish move?

Jellyfish drift along with the tides and currents. They change direction by squeezing their bell-shaped bodies in and out. As they squeeze in, they squirt water out behind them. This pushes the jellyfish through the water.

1 Eel grass	5 Common starfish
2 Greater pipefish	6 Common sea urchin
3 Blenny	7 Goby
4 Scallop	8 Common jellyfish

Now I know...

★ Many fish, such as blennies and gobies, live in the shallows.

★ Jellyfish drift along with the tides and currents.

★ Plaice use camouflage to hide from their enemies.

WHAT is coral?

Look and find ★ ★ starfish

Corals are tiny animals that grow in big **colonies** in the sunny, shallow seas along tropical seashores. Many corals build stony cases to protect themselves. A coral reef is made up of many colonies and grows slowly over thousands of years. It makes a home for many colourful sea creatures.

WHICH animals look like flowers?

Many sea anemones look like exotic flowers, with their petals swaying in the water. In fact, they are jelly-like creatures related to corals and jellyfish. They live on rocks and wave their stinging **tentacles** in the water to catch their food. If prawns or small fish brush against the tentacles, they are paralysed by the stings and pulled into the sea anemones' mouths.

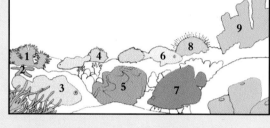

1 Sea anemone	6 Parrot fish
2 Blue starfish	7 Butterfly fish
3 Clown fish	8 Crown-of-
4 Sea fan	thorns starfish
5 Giant clam	9 Sponge

These pieces of coral were once part of a coral reef. They were broken off to be sold to tourists.

WHY are coral reefs in danger?

Coral reefs are being badly damaged by tourist boats, and by people who break them up to use as building material or to sell in tourist shops. Corals can only grow in clean, warm water. Many of them are dying as the sea becomes **polluted** with oil spills and rubbish.

That's Amazing!

Clown fish have a special coat of slime so they can live safely among sea anemones!

Coral reefs grow only about one centimetre a year!

Now I know...

★ Coral reefs are made from large colonies of coral.
★ Sea anemones are tiny animals that look like flowers.
★ Coral reefs are being damaged and destroyed by people.

29

SEASHORE QUIZ

What have you remembered about the seashore? Test what you know and see how much you have learned.

1 How often does the tide go in and out?
a)   once a week
b)   once a day
c)   twice a day

2 Where do kittiwakes build their nests?
a)   on cliff tops
b)   on rocky ledges
c)   on sand dunes

3 Which plants hold sand dunes in place?
a)   seaweeds
b)   grasses
c)   poppies

4 Which shellfish stays in one place for life?
a)   limpet
b)   tellin
c)   barnacle

5 Which animal burrows into rocks?
a)   purple sea urchin
b)   lugworm
c)   cockle

6 Which trees can grow in salty water?
a)   weeping willows
b)   maple trees
c)   mangrove trees

7 Which animals can swim backwards?
a)   crabs
b)   shrimps and prawns
c)   jellyfish

8 What object has a holdfast?
a)   seagull
b)   seaweed
c)   mussel

9 What marks the high tide line?
a)   rocks
b)   grass
c)   seaweed

10 Where do you find coral reefs?
a   in frozen seas
b)   along tropical seashores
c)   on cliffs

Find the answers on page 32.

GLOSSARY

burrows Holes or tunnels in the ground dug and lived in by animals.

byssus threads The tiny threads with which some molluscs attach themselves to rocks.

camouflaged Being coloured in such a way as to match the surrounding area.

colonies Groups of the same animals living together in one place.

coral reefs Colonies of coral found along tropical shores.

driftwood Old, damaged pieces of wood carried onto the seashore by the tides.

estuaries Areas of water where rivers meet the sea.

filter To separate out food from substances such as water.

holdfasts The branched or disc-shaped parts at the bottom of seaweeds with which they grip firmly onto rocks.

mangrove swamps Soft, wet, tropical coastal land covered in mangrove trees. Mangroves have long, tangled underwater roots that support their trunks above water.

migrate To travel from one place to another regularly, usually over long distances, to find food or to mate.

minerals Substances found in rocks, soil, and in the remains of plants and animals.

molluscs Animals that have no backbones and soft bodies protected by hard shells.

polluted Made dirty and harmful by oil, or human or industrial waste.

predators Animals that hunt other animals for food.

prey Animals that are hunted and killed by other animals.

scavengers Animals that eat dead or dying fish and animals.

shingle Small pebbles on a seashore, usually found on the upper parts of the beach.

stranded Washed up and left behind on the seashore.

tentacles The long, bendy parts of sea creatures, such as sea anemones, with which they move about or catch food.

tide The movement of the sea as it comes high up the seashore and goes out again twice every 24 hours.

turf Soil covered in thick, short grass.

31

INDEX

Answers to the Seashore Quiz on page 30
★ 1 c ★ 2 b ★ 3 b ★ 4 c ★ 5 a ★ 6 c ★ 7 b ★ 8 b ★ 9 c ★ 10 b

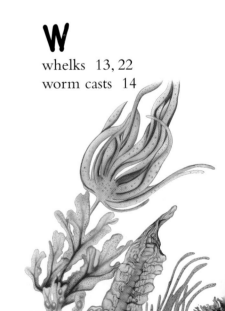